T0127390

THE LITTLE BOOK OF

# CATS

Published by OH!
20 Mortimer Street
London W1T 3JW

Text © 2020 OH!
Design © 2020 OH!

**Disclaimer:**
All trademarks, quotations, company names, registered names, products,
characters, logos and catchphrases used or cited in this book are the property
of their respective owners. This book is a publication of *OH! An imprint
of Welbeck Publishing Group Limited* and has not been licensed, approved,
sponsored, or endorsed by any person or entity. All rights reserved. No part
of this publication may be reproduced, stored in a retrieval system, or
transmitted in any form or by any means (including electronic, mechanical,
photocopying, recording, or otherwise) without prior written permission
from the publisher.

ISBN 978-1-91161-094-6

Editorial: Stella Caldwell
Project manager: Russell Porter
Design: Tony Seddon
Production: Rachel Burgess

A CIP catalogue record for this book is available from the British Library

Printed in China

10 9 8 7 6 5 4

Illustrations: Shutterstock

# THE LITTLE BOOK OF
# CATS

PURRS OF WISDOM

# CONTENTS

# INTRODUCTION

Cats and dogs have long vied for victory in the best furry friend battle. Dog lovers insist upon their pet's sociability, loyalty and unconditional affection. Cats, they often argue, are aloof, selfish and only in it for the food.

But as any cat lover will tell you, cats do develop real bonds with their human owners. And while it's true they are independent rather than pack animals, for many people that's the point. As well as being curious and playful companions, cats are clean-living and low-maintenance – and let's not forget another thing: they *purr*. Is there anything more soothing than the sound and feel of a vibrating cat on your lap?

Descended from African wild cats, *Felis catus* has been in a relationship with humans for thousands of years. The oldest archaeological evidence for domestication can be traced back to the Mediterranean island of Cyprus, where a 9,500-year old burial site containing the remains of a cat and its probable owner was discovered. Then, of course, it's well known that the ancient Egyptians not only prized cats as rodent-catchers and cherished companions, but also revered them as sacred creatures.

Today, we may joke that cats have never forgotten the days when they were worshipped. Perhaps it's that haughty, entitled look they have perfected, or the way they really do seem to call the shots. But as anyone who has succumbed to their bewitching charms knows, cats have a way of working their paw-prints into our hearts and making themselves right at home.

Including quotes from across the ages alongside fascinating facts and tidbits, this delightful Little Book of feline wit and wisdom pays homage to the pawsome cat and reminds us why time spent with them is "never wasted".

CHAPTER
## ONE

# WHY
# CATS
# RULE

They
# NEVER
bark

They are
# masters
of
# stealth
and the
# high jump

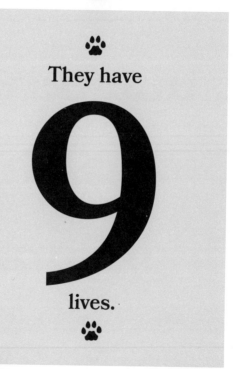

They have

9

lives.

# Their bellies are like

# soft dough

They are
**easy to
entertain**
with paper, boxes and
**string**

# They
# **purr**

CHAPTER
TWO

# FABULOUS
# FELINES

"The smallest feline is a masterpiece."

Leonardo da Vinci

wanted body
and life, which is why it
turned into a

"I value in the cat the independent and almost ungrateful spirit which prevents her from attaching herself to any one... When we caress her, she stretches herself and arches her back responsively; but this is because she feels an agreeable sensation, not because she takes a silly satisfaction, like the dog, in faithfully loving a thankless master."

François-René
de Chateaubriand

The love of cats
is called

# ailurophilia

from the Greek

*ailuros* ("cat") and

*philia* ("love").

**"I** have studied many philosophers and many cats. The wisdom of cats is infinitely superior."

Hippolyte Taine

"If animals could speak, the dog would be a blundering outspoken fellow; but the cat would have the rare grace of never saying a word too much."

Mark Twain

I used to

# love

dogs – until I
discovered

# cats.

In ancient Egypt, the cat goddess **Bastet** was depicted as a woman with a cat's head, and was associated with **happiness** and **comfort**. When a sacred cat died, its body was **mummified** and placed in a special tomb.

**"I** believe cats to be spirits come to earth. A cat, I am sure, could walk on a cloud without coming through.**"**

Jules Verne

"Ablack cat among roses,
Phlox, lilac-misted under a first-
quarter moon,
The sweet smells of heliotrope and
night-scented stock.
The garden is very still,
It is dazed with moonlight,
Contented with perfume,
Dreaming the opium dreams of its
folded poppies."

Amy Lowell, "The Garden by Moonlight"

"Time spent with cats is never wasted."

Sigmund Freud

"**K**ind old ladies assure us that cats are often the best judges of character. A cat will always go to a good man, they say…"

Virginia Woolf, *Jacob's Room*, 1922

"**P**rowling his own
quiet backyard or asleep
by the fire, [the cat] is still
only a whisker away from
the wilds."

Jean Burden

Over the centuries,
the cat has travelled
the world and
been introduced to
countries like

Australia,

where there
were previously
no cats.

"There are two means of refuge from the miseries of life: music and cats."

Albert Schweitzer

"The kitten has a luxurious, Bohemian, unpuritanical nature. It eats six meals a day, plays furiously with a toy mouse and a piece of rope, and suddenly falls into a deep sleep whenever the fit takes it. It never feels the necessity to do anything to justify its existence…"

Robertson Davies, *The Diary of Samuel Marchbanks*, 1947

The more people
I meet, the more
I love my

# cat.

"The cat does not offer services. The cat offers itself."

William S. Burroughs, *The Cat Inside*, 1986

Today, there
are more than

# 500
# million

domestic cats
in the world.

"A cat's rage is beautiful, burning with pure cat flame, all its hair standing up and crackling blue sparks, eyes blazing and sputtering."

William S. Burroughs,
*The Cat Inside*, 1986

"It is impossible to keep a straight face in the presence of one or more kittens."

Cynthia E. Vernado

"In ancient times, cats were worshipped as gods. They have never forgotten this."

Terry Pratchett

"I
think that the
world should be full of cats and full
    of rain,
that's all, just
cats and
rain, rain and cats, very nice, good
night."

Charles Bukowski, *Betting on the Muse:*
*Poems and Stories*, 1996

# Cats are made to store

caresses

Cats have **five toes**
on each of their front
paws, and **four toes**
on the back paws.
It's not unusual
for cats to have **extra
toes**, though!

"Having a bunch of cats around is good. If you're feeling bad, just look at the cats, you'll feel better, because they know that everything is, just as it is."

Charles Bukowski,
*On Cats*, 2015

"A kitten is, in the animal world, what a rosebud is in the garden."

Robert Sowthey

**"I**f there were to be a universal sound depicting peace, I would surely vote for the purr."

Barbara L. Diamond

**"I** have lived with several Zen masters – all of them cats.**"**

Eckhart Tolle, *The Power of Now:*
*A Guide to Spiritual Enlightenment*, 2001

# Cats
# **rule**
# and dogs
# **drool.**

Unlike dogs,
cats don't have a
**sweet tooth**
– and chocolate
is strictly off the
menu!

"Dogs believe they are human. Cats believe they are God."

Jeff Valdez

A group of cats
is called a
clowder,
while a group of kittens
is called a
kindle?

"**C**ats will outsmart dogs every time."

John Grogan

CHAPTER

# THREE

# COMPANION-
# SHIP

"I recollect him one day scrambling up Dr Johnson's breast, apparently with much satisfaction... and when I observed he was a fine cat, saying, 'why yes, Sir, but I have had cats whom I liked

better than this;' and then,
as if perceiving Hodge to be
out of countenance, adding,
'but he is a very fine cat, a
very fine cat indeed.'"

James Boswell, *Life of Samuel Johnson*, 1791

Cats can make up to

# 100

**different sounds,**
from miaows and purrs
to chirps and yowls –
and many nuanced
variations in between.

"**W**hat greater gift than
the love of a cat."

Charles Dickens

"A home without a cat – and a well-fed, well-petted and properly revered cat – may be a perfect home, perhaps, but how can it prove title?"

Mark Twain, *Pudd'nhead Wilson*, 1894

# Home
is where the
## cat is.

"Cats know how to obtain food without labour, shelter without confinement, and love without penalties."

W.L. George

"**A** house isn't a home without the ineffable contentment of a cat with its tail folded about its feet. A cat gives mystery, charm, suggestion."

L.M. Montgomery,
*Emily's Quest,* 1927

Even an active cat spends
two-thirds of its day snoozing!
That means a nine-year old
cat will have spent

# 3
## years

of its life asleep...

# No outfit is **complete** without cat **hairs!**

"A garden without cats, it will be generally agreed, can scarcely deserve to be called a garden at all... Much of the magic of the heather beds would vanish if, as we bent over them, there was no chance that we might hear a faint rustle among the blossoms, and find ourselves staring into a pair of sleepy green eyes."

Beverley Nichols, *Garden Open Tomorrow*, 1968

"**P**erhaps God made cats so that man might have the pleasure of fondling the tiger..."

Robertson Davies, *The Diary of Samuel Marchbanks*, 1947

"There are few things in life more heart-warming than to be welcomed by a cat."

Tay Hohoff

**"There is something about the presence of a cat... that seems to take the bite out of being alone."**

Louis J. Camuti

Cats can be right-pawed
or left-pawed.
**Female** cats are more
likely to favour the
**right paw**, while **male**
cats more often use
their **left** paw.

**"I** have felt cats rubbing their face against mine and touching my cheek with claws gently sheathed. These things, to me, are expressions of love.**"**

James Herriot

The *cat's* in charge, I just *pay the rent.*

"Cats have it all –
admiration, an endless sleep,
and company only when
they want it."

Rod McKuen

"No man or woman can be called friendless who has the companionship of a cat."

James Lautner

"**A**uthors like cats because they are such quiet, lovable, wise creatures, and cats like authors for the same reasons."

Robertson Davies

President
Abraham Lincoln
was a big fan
of cats. When his
wife was once asked
if he had any hobbies,
she replied

# "cats!"

Anything is
# **paw-sible**
with a cat
by your side.

"Cats do care. For example, they know instinctively what time we have to be at work in the morning and they wake us up twenty minutes before the alarm goes off."

Michael Nelson

"Cats come and go
without ever leaving."

Martha Curtis

# "Cats don't have friends. They have co-conspirators."

Darby Conley, *Get Fuzzy* comic, 31 May 2015

"I love my cats more than I love most people. Probably more than is healthy."

Amy Lee

························

CHAPTER

FOUR

# CATTITUDE

"When I am playing with my cat, how do I know she is not playing with me?"

Michel de Montaigne, *Essais de Michel de Montaigne*, 1580

"Curiosity killed the cat."

Ben Jonson, *Every Man in His Humour*, 1598

Cats' eyes have a
**reflective**
layer, which
helps them to see
**in the dark.**
This layer
glows green when
light strikes it.

"**A**rise from sleep, old cat,
And with great yawns and
stretchings...
Amble out for love."

Issa Kobayashi, Japanese Haiku

"It is difficult to obtain the friendship of a cat. It is a philosophical animal... one that does not place its affections thoughtlessly."

Théophile Gautier

*Cattitude* is everything.

"Cats are mysterious kind of folk. There is more passing in their minds than we are aware of. It comes no doubt from their being so familiar with warlocks and witches."

Sir Walter Scott

**"T**he ideal of calm exists in a sitting cat.**"**

Jules Renard

A cat's heart
beats

two to three

times faster
than
a human's.

She
**came,**
she

*purred,*

she
**conquered.**

"Of all God's creatures, there is only one that cannot be made slave of the leash. That one is the cat. If man could be crossed with the cat it would improve the man, but it would deteriorate the cat."

Mark Twain

"I love them, they are so nice and selfish. Dogs are TOO good and unselfish. They make me feel uncomfortable. But cats are gloriously human."

L.M. Montgomery,
*Anne of the Island*, 1915

**66** 'And how do you know that
you're mad?'

'To begin with,' said the Cat, 'a
dog's not mad. You grant that?'

'I suppose so,' said Alice…

…'Well then,' the Cat went on, 'you
see a dog growls when it's angry,
and wags its tail when it's pleased.

Now I growl when I'm pleased,
and wag my tail when I'm angry.
Therefore I'm mad.'

'I call it purring, not growling,'
said Alice.

'Call it what you like,' said the Cat."

Lewis Carroll,
*Alice's Adventures
in Wonderland,*
1865

In 1963,

# Félicette

became the first and
only cat astronaut
when she was
launched into space
for 15 minutes by
French scientists.

"**O**ne cat just leads to another."

Letter from Ernest Hemingway to his first wife,
Elizabeth Hadley Richardson, 1943

"The city of cats and the city of men exist one inside the other, but they are not the same city."

Italo Calvino

# After dark, all cats are **leopards.**

"Throw a stick, and the servile dog wheezes and pants and stumbles to bring it to you. Do the same before a cat, and he will eye you with coolly polite and somewhat bored amusement. And just as inferior people prefer the inferior animal which scampers excitedly because someone else wants something...

… so do superior people respect
the superior animal which lives its
own life and knows that the puerile
stick-throwings of alien bipeds
are none of its business and beneath
its notice."

H.P. Lovecraft,
*Something About Cats and Other Pieces,* 1949

The average cat litter produces three to five kittens. The largest known litter consisted of

# 19

## kittens,

of which **15** survived.

"Are cats strange animals
or do they so resemble us
that we find them curious as
we do monkeys?"

John Steinbeck, *The Winter
of Our Discontent*, 1961

"**W**ork – other people's work – is an intolerable idea to a cat. Can you picture cats herding sheep or agreeing to pull a cart? They will not inconvenience themselves to the slightest degree."

Louis J. Camuti, Lloyd Alexander,
*Park Avenue Vet*, 1962

A cat has nine lives.

For **three** he plays,

for **three** he strays

and for the last **three**
he stays.

"**W**omen and cats will do as they please, and men and dogs should relax and get used to the idea."

Robert A. Heinlein

**"I**t always gives me a shiver when I see a cat seeing what I can't see."

Eleanor Farjeon,
*Faithful Jenny Dove: And
Other Illusions*, 1963

A cat's vision
is similar to that
of a human
who is colour blind –
red shades
probably appear as
green
to your cat.

"Cats are inquisitive,
but hate to admit it."

Mason Cooley

"One reason that cats are happier than people is that they have no newspapers."

Gwendolyn Brooks, *In the Mecca*, 1968

Sometimes
you just have to
 *paws*
and *relax.*

"Let us be honest: most of us rather like our cats to have a streak of wickedness. I should not feel quite easy in the company of any cat that walked around the house with a saintly expression."

Beverley Nichols, *Cats A Z*, 1977

“Like all pure creatures, cats are practical.”

William S. Burroughs, *The Cat Inside*, 1986

Adult cats **rarely miaow** to each other – they reserve that sound for **communicating with humans** (especially when they want food!) Cats communicate with fellow felines using **body language**, **scent** and a **range of other sounds.**

"Nothing divided people more deeply than how they felt about cats."

Kingsley Amis, *Difficulties with Girls*, 1988

# In a
# **cat's eye,**

## all things belong to cats.

'I meant,' said Ipslore bitterly, 'what is there in this world that truly makes living worthwhile?'

Death thought about it.

'CATS,' he said eventually. 'CATS ARE NICE.'"

Terry Pratchett, *Sourcery*, 1988

"Cats are connoisseurs of comfort."

James Herriot, *James Herriot's Cat Stories*, 1994

"Meow means woof in cat."

George Carlin

Most cats hate water
but the
# Turkish Van
is an exception
– unlike other cats, its
coat has a unique texture
that makes it unusually
water-repellent.

"A cat will do what it wants when it wants, and there's not a thing you can do about it."

Frank Perkins

"Witches were a bit like cats. They didn't much like one another's company, but they did like to know where all the other witches were, just in case they needed them."

Terry Pratchett, *A Hat Full of Sky*, 2004

There is no

# snooze

button on a
cat that wants
breakfast.

"As every cat owner knows, nobody owns a cat."

Ellen Perry Berkeley

"The problem with cats is that they get the same exact look whether they see a moth or an axe-murderer."

Paula Poundstone

The oldest cat
on record is
**Crème Puff**
from Austin, Texas.
Born in 1967,
she died in 2005 at the
grand old age of

# 38.

"Dogs have their day but cats have 365."

Lilian Jackson Braun

I'm glad
my cat can't
**talk,**
he
**knows**
too much.

“When Rome burned,
the emperor's cats still
expected to be fed on time.”

Seanan McGuire, *Rosemary and Rue*, 2010

"I would like to see anyone, prophet, king or God, convince a thousand cats to do the same thing at the same time."

Neil Gaiman

"**S**leep is like a cat: it only comes to you if you ignore it."

Gillian Flynn

CHAPTER

FIVE

# PAWS
# FOR
# THOUGHT

It's true that cats aren't too keen on taking lessons from us – but that doesn't detract from the fact there's plenty we can learn from observing our fluffy companions!

# Be curious

Cats were born to explore,
and although they
occasionally find themselves
in a spot of bother it keeps
things exciting! Tap into
your adventurous spirit and
take advantage of all the world
has to offer you.

# Do what makes you happy

Cats don't waste time fretting about what they should be doing (or haven't done). They sleep, eat, bird-watch, pounce, and then sleep again. And it makes them happy. Find out what you like doing, and go for it!

# Learn to chill

Whether stretched out in front of a fire or curled up tight in a sunny flowerpot, cats are masters of zen. They don't fret about yesterday or tomorrow – and they look pretty good on it!

# Take time to stare

Have you ever noticed
how a cat will happily sit at
a window gazing at the
world outside?
Cats are in tune with their
surroundings, and they
take time to study the
little details.

# Stretch regularly

Been sitting at your desk too long? Like little yogis, cats know just how important a good stretch is — it keeps their bodies limber and feels amazing.

# Look your best

When they're not sleeping, cats spend a lot of time cleaning themselves. As the old saying goes, cleanliness is next to godliness – and it can't be a bad thing if we make sure we're always well groomed!

# Be hard to get!

Cats don't play hard to get –
they are hard to get!
They don't waste any time
sucking up to people they
don't like but when they give
their affection to a human
friend, they mean it.

# Enjoy the simple things

You can buy your pet a state-of-the-art cat toy if you like, but you can bet your kitty will be just as happy playing with a piece of rustling paper or a cardboard box.
Who needs the latest gizmos? Take pleasure in life's simple things.

# Go crazy once in a while

Cats are great at taking life easy, but every now and then, they get that wild look in their eyes and the slightest movement puts them in pounce mode. We all know that feeling when we need to let off steam – go for it!

# CHAPTER
# SIX

# PURRS
## OF
# WISDOM

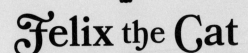

is widely
considered to be the
first animated film star,
first appearing in

# 1919.

**"I**n nine lifetimes, you'll never know as much about your cat as your cat knows about you.**"**

Michel de Montaigne

"Those who'll play with cats must expect to be scratched."

Miguel de Cervantes, *Don Quixote*, 1605–15

"**N**othing's more playful than a young cat, nor more grave than an old one."

Thomas Fuller, *Gnomologia*, 1732

"The cat lives alone. He has no need of society. He obeys only when he wishes, he pretends to sleep the better to see, and scratches everything he can scratch."

François-René de Chateaubriand

# Dogs have owners, cats have staff.

In just
seven years, a
single female cat
or "queen"
and her offspring
could produce

# 420,000

cats.

"A cat will be your friend,
but never your slave."

Théophile Gautier

# Top 5
## Biggest Cat Breeds

These cuddly companions give
you a lot more cat to love!

1. **Maine Coone**

2. **Savannah**

3. **Ragdoll**

4. **Chausie**

5. **Ragamuffin**

"The cat is, above all things, a dramatist; its life is lived in an endless romance though the drama is played out on quite another stage than our own…"

Margaret Benson, *The Soul of a Cat and Other Stories*, 1901

"Every household should contain a cat, not only for decorative and domestic values, but because the cat in quiescence is medicinal to irritable, tense, tortured men and women."

William Lyon Phelps

**"There are no ordinary cats."**

Colette

Most cats are
crazy about catnip,
a herb belonging to the
mint family.
Catnip contains

# nepetalactone,

a chemical compound
that gives cats a high
when sniffed!

"A cat has absolute emotional honesty: human beings, for one reason or another, may hide their feelings, but a cat does not."

Ernest Hemingway

"The Naming of cats is a
difficult matter;
It isn't just one of your holiday games.
You may think at first, I'm as mad
as a hatter
When I tell you a cat must have
THREE DIFFERENT NAMES."

T.S. Eliot, "The Naming of Cats", *Old Possum's
Book of Practical Cats*, 1939

You can
# TEACH A CAT
to do anything

(that it
wants to do).

"Cats are smarter than dogs. You can't get eight cats to pull a sled through snow."

Jeff Valdez

"Dogs are like kids. Cats are like roommates."

Oliver Gaspirtz

A cat's
sense of smell
is incredibly
sensitive, and
up to

# 14 times

more powerful than
a human's.

"A cat does not want all the world to love her. Only those she has chosen to love."

Helen Thomson

"Cats have lived as solitary hunters for most of their ancestry… So what we may interpret as 'aloofness' or 'indifference' is really just self-sufficiency – …

... a self reliance that has been in their genes and stood them in good stead for centuries."

Tracie Hotchner, *The Cat Bible*, 2007

"I think all cats are wild. They only act tame if there's a saucer of milk in it for them."

Douglas Adams, *Last Chance to See*, 1991

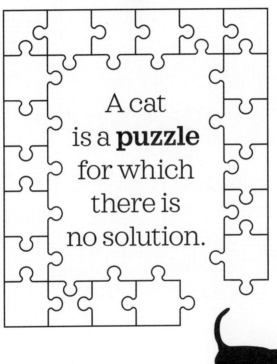

A cat
is a **puzzle**
for which
there is
no solution.

A cat's
**whiskers**
are extensions of
its skin. They can detect
even the smallest change
in the environment
and help cats to judge
the width of gaps.

"Never try to outstubborn a cat."

Robert A. Heinlein, *Time Enough for Love*, 1973

"The way to get on with a cat is to treat it as an equal – or even better, as the superior it knows itself to be."

Elizabeth Peters,
*The Snake, the Crocodile and the Dog*, 1992

Climbing a tree
is optional –

coming down
is not.

"You never choose a cat. He chooses you."

Philippe Ragueneau

"I am a cat. We aren't required to make sense."

Seanan McGuire

A cat's tail tells plenty of tales about its mood!

An **upright** tail held high expresses **confidence**, a **twitching** tail indicates a **watchful** cat, while a **puffed up** bristling tail is a sign of **aggression**.

# Real
# men like
# *cats.*

"A lie is like a cat: you need to stop it before it gets out the door or it's really hard to catch."

Charles M. Blow

Happiness is
falling asleep
to the sound of
your cat
**purring.**

"Way down deep,
we're all motivated by the
same urges. Cats have the
courage to live by them."

Jim Davis

People who
don't like

# cats

were probably

mice

in an earlier life.

A cat can rotate
its ears
# 180 degrees,
allowing them to tune
into the faintest squeak
or rustling noise. They
can hear higher-pitched
sounds than humans
and most dogs.

"Cats are intended to teach us that not everything in nature has a purpose."

Garrison Keillor

"The cat could very well
be man's best friend but
would never stoop to
admitting it."

Douglas Larson

Cats can

# purrrrrr

their
way out
of anything.

# Oldest Cat Breeds

**1. Egyptian Mau** – it is estimated the Mau's ancestors were first recorded in ancient Egypt, around 4,000 years ago.

**2. Norwegian Forest Cat** – this fluffy feline's ancestors were brought to Norway by the Vikings over 1,000 years ago.

**3. Siamese** – this popular breed descended from the sacred temple cats in the kingdom of Siam (modern-day Thailand), as early as the 1350s.

**"I**t is a truth universally acknowledged that a man in possession of a warm house and a well-stocked fridge must be in want of a cat.**"**

Heather Hacking,
*How Cats Conquered The World,*
2004

"The only thing a cat worries about is what's happening right now. As we tell the kittens, you can only wash one paw at a time."

Lloyd Alexander, *Time Cat*, 1963

"Purr more, hiss less."

Linda C. Marchman

Have a mice day!